LOST LAGOON
lost in thought

Caitlin Press Inc.
8100 Alderwood Road,
Halfmoon Bay, BC V0N 1Y1
www.caitlin-press.com

Text and cover design by Vici Johnstone
Cover photo by Tracey Tomtene
Printed in Canada

Caitlin Press Inc. acknowledges financial support from the Government of Canada and the Canada Council for the Arts, and the Province of British Columbia through the British Columbia Arts Council and the Book Publisher's Tax Credit.
Library and Archives Canada Cataloguing in Publication

Lost lagoon/lost in thought : prose poems / Betsy Warland.
Warland, Betsy, 1946- author.
Canadiana 20190204303 | ISBN 9781773860251 (softcover)
LCGFT: Poetry.
LCC PS8595.A7745 L67 2020 | DDC C811/.54—dc23

LOST LAGOON

lost in thought

prose poems

BETSY WARLAND

Caitlin Press

With gratitude and respect, I dedicate this book to Pauline (Canada's first performance artist and Indigenous poet), Jean (the Beaver Lady of Lost Lagoon), and Fiona (the Swan Lady of Lost Lagoon).

The Notebook

The net of belief we throw over one another
finding it ever empty
or ensnared
with what we didn't want.

Baited line
beachcomber of
  belief—
a tear of gratitude
the only reliable measure.

The buoy of belief

Nothing more perilous than eyes
that once embraced you.

Copious kelptongues of belief—
shushing any outcry
as you're pulled down
be leaf
belie
  beleag—

To be without belief

Curious
as the harbour seal surfacing in front of you
a tender memory
of something vital in its face
you have forgotten.

Contents

Acknowledgements

I want to acknowledge and express my gratitude and respect to the Squamish, Musqueam, Tsleil-Waututh, and Burrard Inlet peoples upon whose ancestral, ceremonial and unceded lands I have written *Lost Lagoon/lost in thought* and whose 10,000 years of living on the Salish Sea Coast informed and enriched this book.

Also, I want to thank the British Columbia Arts Council for a grant that enabled a period of crucial writing time that I needed for *Lost Lagoon/lost in thought*.

The Human is at a loss for words

The Human is at a loss for words. Considers. And, considers. Wonders, is this loss of words perhaps why The Human is a writer? The desire to describe something that The Human cherishes makes words scatter like a flock of startled bushtits. The very word "cherishes" is suspect. Passé.

Okay, The Human thinks (again), let's begin with its name: Lost Lagoon. Its very name is a conundrum. How can one misplace a lagoon? Standing on the shore any passerby can observe it's not a lagoon but a small lake or, perhaps, a pond.

Over the decades, The Human has walked around the lagoon chatting with various companions, but now dwelling close to it, lives with it. The difference between "around" and "with." Difference between pointing with camera, voice or index finger, and standing still—watching, listening, sniffing, occasionally speaking softly or returning a bird's call.

Just across the street from the high- and low-rise buildings' cheek and jowlness, Lost Lagoon life is_____.
Once again, The Human is at a loss for words.

The lagoon resists being depicted. Summed up. The Human admires this.

#2

That said, under the cover of darkness and human absence,

That said, under the cover of darkness and human absence, the lagoon spills into surrounding life. Many are the nights that The Human is jolted awake by alarmed quacking of geese and ducks. Coyote, owl, or otter on the prowl have startled them: their panic echoes inside The Human's head.

#3

During every six o'clock news commercial

During every six o'clock news commercial break The Human and Son mimic the cartoon-like female voice singing "Everyone Loves Marine Land" that accompanies footage of synchronized ballet jumps by trained beluga whales in an unintentional parody of human folly.

Less than a minute away from this low-rise building, Lost Lagoon dwellers keep their distance. You might disagree. What about all those photos of raccoons, Canada geese, mallards, and chickadees coming to cupped hands? Most lagoon dwellers do not.

Disregard, wariness, and retreat prevail when we are near.

#4

Geese hold their ground even through

Geese hold their ground even through their numerous, routine naps—switch to unihemispheric sleeping mode (one lidded eye in deep sleep the other in vigilant alert) as effortlessly as the humans switch apps on their phones.

#5

The Human became engrossed by

The Human became engrossed by the neighbourhood crows before moving here. Was intrigued by their routine flight overhead early morn to their countless territories of waking life, and eve returning to their Burnaby roost. Now, they don't just pass over but they dwell, and The Human has learned the subtle differences between each crow's caw (khaaw-khaa, caw-cah, kahr-kahr, caar-caar); on a Google search, they have thirty different calls.

Most mornings, The Human listens for the leader's first emphatic caw-caw to check all are accounted for and can now begin their workday. In pre-twilight, when they gather on two of the high-rises' curved balconies across the street, none depart until all members of the flock have arrived.

The Human has learned that the nestlings plummet to the ground and learn to walk. Then, fly. Learned that crows make tools to reach food; recent research confirms crow brains are far more similar to chimpanzees' than to other birds' brains.

As crows flourish between the apartment buildings and Stanley Park's 400 hectares, The Human (a person of between) flourishes between these opposite yet interdependent worlds.

Occasionally, The Human feeds neighbourhood crows; alerts them with three resonant clicks on roof of mouth then spreads leftover meat scraps on a large tree stump nearby. Sometimes, when too much time has passed, they give a sidelong, quizzical look. Then The Human whispers, "Yes, tomorrow."

One yearling recently followed The Human up to building's door. This intimacy surprised. Whispering, The Human remembered "Yes, sorry, you're right. I forgot. Tomorrow for sure." Crow (quickly) studied The Human's face then, satisfied the promise would be kept, flew away.

#6

Have the neighbourhood crows named

Have the neighbourhood crows named The Human? Possibly,
considering their impressive vocabulary. Although this notion is
initially appealing, The Human sighs at the thought.

Considers.

Then realizes it's a relief to have no given name. No surname.
Liberating to be unbound by painstakingly constructed (and
defended) human identity with all its self-replicating specificity.

In life in and around Lost Lagoon, it's likely that The Human is
not perceived as she, he, or I. Rather, is inevitably and irreversibly
perceived as generically human. In the natural world we are
awkwardly, self-consciously, often dangerously (The) Human(s).

When non-indigenous humans use the phrase "the natural
world," most often we're referring to all forms of non-human life
not man-made for we believe ourselves not part of the natural
world but masters of it.

This is our human condition.

In the spring, The Human happened upon

In the spring, The Human happened upon a strange sight on the lagoon. Two swans, a few feet from the shore, faced each other, held their necks and heads together creating the shape of a heart. One then curved its neck over the other's and both simultaneously dipped and submerged heads and necks up to their bodies then raised their heads into the same position and repeated this elegant gesture numerous times.

Mesmerized, The Human wondered: "Is this a mating ritual?" Later, found out it was.

This exquisiteness now resides within The Human.

A year later, looking up the etymological root of *swan*, The Human discovers it shares the Latin root with *sonnet* and *sonata*.

#8

For years, decades in fact, whenever visiting

For years, decades in fact, whenever visiting Stanley Park, The Human puzzled over its name: Lost Lagoon. How did it get this nonsensical name? It seemed an oxymoron or a Zen koan. Then water drove The Human to water. The apartment flooded, and The Human moved here.

Just like the magnetism of the river four kilometres away from the family farm, Lost Lagoon magnetized The Human. Now, this close proximity has provoked an investigation into its curious name.

One might guess that it was named by a poet. Indeed it was. E. Pauline Johnson, part Mohawk part English, was fond of paddling her canoe there when it was a quiet cove. Here a "however" hovers. With summer tides, during Johnson's favoured paddling time, her refuge was temporarily lost.

Then, was lost permanently in 1916 when construction of the Stanley Park causeway cut the cove off from the sea. Lost, too, for the Skwxwú7mesh / Squamish, Musxʷməθkwəy'əm / Musqueam and Səl'ílwətaʔ/Selilwitulh / Burrard nations' peoples who harvested clams and other sea life from the mudflats for generations, probably centuries.

"*Lost*, leu, to loosen, divide, cut apart." The causeway separating the sea and the tidal flat.

"*Lost*, leu-, forleasan, to forfeit," these unceded territories of the Indigenous Peoples.

Lost, another word for

taken.

#9

The Human's first intimacy with a pond

The Human's first intimacy with a pond was third hand: words in a journal that eventually became words printed on the pages of Henry David Thoreau's *Walden; or, Life in the Woods* that The Human read as a teenager. Thoreau's book embodied a way of thinking and living that elated a solitary Midwestern farm Child.

On the farm there was no pond. So, The Child began studying the array of life held inside the cattle's cement water trough. Like a mammal or bird, The Child built secret hideouts dotting a radius of four kilometres. Then ventured further away, travelling first by foot, then pony and eventually bike, The Child's water refuges were the dredge ditch (800 metres), river and woods (four kilometres).

The operative word here is "away."

The Child fled whenever possible.

Humans' duplicity was not only troubling—their lack of awareness about it made them dangerous. The Child watched. Considered.

Saw the harm inflicted on one another was considerable, but the harm inflicted on nature was ruthless.

#10
Thoreau began felling trees

Thoreau began felling trees to build his cabin in March, 1845. Pauline Johnson was born 1861. As paddling gave Pauline refuge, Thoreau could free himself from "this restless, nervous, bustling, trivial Nineteen Century" at Walden.

In some respects, the way of the world feels much the same as it did one hundred and seventy-one years ago. Just now The Human inserted earplugs to muffle the relentless bass of the sound system throbbing in the building next door; the lawnmower's roar beneath the apartment window.

In the early 70s, The Human made a pilgrimage to Walden and was taken aback. Concord, and its proliferating suburbs, noosed Walden. Only a narrow collar of woods separated it from domestic and commercial buildings' robust activities and "trucks rumbling loudly down Route 126."

Lost Lagoon? It has fared a bit better.

Highway 99 is on the east, tennis courts and high-rises on the south, but the stream and meadow on the west and forest on the north remain. Further improvement schemes to fill the lagoon in to create a sports field, build a stadium on the north and museum on the south, build a man-made island in the middle for Theatre of the Stars and boat audiences back and forth have not been implemented.

Thoreau's mantra was "simplify, simplify."

Concord resident and Thoreauvian Tom Blanding observes that if Walden visitors find the photo-snapping crowds, bathhouse frolic and traffic din "disappointing, that's because Walden is true. It shows where our society stands in relation to nature."

#11
The Human ponders. Does a Google search.

The Human ponders. Does a Google search. Yes: there it is.
In 1861, 84 percent of Canadians dwelled in rural areas. By 2015,
80 percent of Canadians dwelled in urban areas. Recent census
figures indicate we are nearing 90 percent.

In two hundred years—a complete reversal—the coin of our
collective consciousness flipped. Forgetting we have forgotten our
deep relationship, reliance on nature, nature has become scenic
background to our playlists (at best); monetized and expendable
(at worst).

Recently, four of The Human's friends (three of whom are writers)
have been curious to read these *Lost Lagoon* pieces. One controversy
arose: two responded positively to the narrator being named The
Human; two found it frustrating, wanted it replaced with I, she, or
Betsy. This signaled the necessity for The Human to address this
nomenclature debate with you (yes, "dear reader").

The usage of "he" typically applied to all nonhumans whose gender
is not evident—pronouns used routinely for animals and insects
as well humans—suggests a commonality, equality, which belies
our assumptions and actions (of superiority). The signifier of
"she" for a woman and "she" for a female mallard fail to signal this
profound disjunction. And, the given name Betsy falls away in the
natural world: becomes meaningless. Then there's the champ: "I."
In The Human's seventy-first year, The Human is weary of North
Americans' obsessive use of "I" which has rendered this pronoun
meaningless.

Bankrupt.

#12

Wakefulness in the night.

Wakefulness in the night.

The Human ponders benefits of nocturnal life: how hunting
owls are free from the eagles' glaring gaze; how beaver turn sweet
bark branches like cobs of corn and chew loudly; how the
skunks saunter without compunction as we make way; how bat
choreography laces the insect-take-out-food air, how darkness
changes everything as striving of most living things abates.

Then The Human considers how the proportions of humans to
all other life feels more easeful and balanced in the depth of the
night or on major holidays when the city empties out.

Additional thoughts about nocturnal life current through The
Human's mind as does Vita Sackville-West's White Garden at
Sissinghurst; The Human visited there in 2008.

Insomnia—curse of countless humans' nights—inspired Vita's
vision of a white garden comprised solely of white blooms and
pale grey foliage that would be illuminated by the moon, a garden
that shone in darkness. That invited in-the-middle-of-the-night-
free-of-time-and-tasks-strolls to lull the mind.

"I cannot help
hoping that the
great ghostly barn
owl will sweep
silently across…the pale
garden that I am
now planting under
the first flakes of
snow. It is magical."

Vita Sackville-West

#13

By mid-February the bare branches

By mid-February the bare branches of the horse chestnut, cottonwood and alder became an airy orchestra pit reverberant with their "liquid gurgling" ascending song. The Human, drawn out of her apartment, searched for the source. Knew who but couldn't believe that red-winged blackbirds would be here. Cautioning herself that she must be imagining it, The Human walked north along the shoreline of the lagoon, her body humming with excitement. The increasingly loud raucous, unfurling chorus pulled The Human eastward to Chilco and Robson. There! In the massive cottonwood, smaller alder and nearby arms-flung-open horse chestnut, hundreds were alighted on every branch. It was them! Them! Decades and decades had passed without their unbridled exuberance. As a solitary girl, The Child would travel by horse or bike to their favoured territory. Although "the stream" was a manmade dredge ditch to drain rainwater standing in the fields, it inadvertently became a rare sanctuary for wildlife. Its diagonal line the only one in a grid of straight ones in every direction for hundreds of kilometres.

Wildlife had been almost eradicated by farmers optimizing productivity of one of the best black-black soils in the world. Nearly every tree removed. Upon arriving at the dredge ditch, the red-winged blackbirds' song never failed to acknowledge arrival of The Child: this her only hearty welcome home greeting. In that narrow slice of wildness, The Child studied the stream life of muskrat, frogs, minnow, turtles, insects, field mice, hawk, and songbirds. Every few years the farmers would "clean up the dredge ditch." Get rid of all tall grasses and small saplings and muskrat lodges. Sometimes do controlled burning. The Child would plead with her father but to no avail. Eventually, the wild ones would reclaim it.

Now. Here. In The Human's seventieth year, between the lagoon, forest, and the grid of high- and low-rises, The Human is saturated with their lusty, jubilant song. Once again made whole. Sound.

Welcomed home.

#14

After many years of meager sunlight

After many years of meager sunlight-infused apartments, The
Human luxuriates in the four-and-a-half-south-facing windows
of her new rental. After moving in, The Human noticed a crow
couple that routinely perched on a pair of two-metre high flag-
poles atop the low-rise across the street. Contentment emanated
from these crows (who typically mate for life) as they observed
life around them. Their shared interval repeated numerous times
throughout the day. Its quiet tenderness reassured The Human.

On the second summer, a crow alarm and commotion issued
from below. The Human scanned outside her windows but did
not spot anything. A few hours later, going out to fetch groceries,
The Human noticed a stark blackness on the green of her low-
rise: a dead crow. It startled The Human. Saddened her. As crows
have their rituals about death, The Human did not touch it. It
remained there a couple of days before the building caretaker
removed it.

By then, The Human had noticed only one crow perched on the
flagpoles but The Human coddled the hope that she had failed
to glimpse them both in their reverie there. Each day, the solitary
crow sat on the same pole. The other pole throbbed its emptiness.

Did the remaining crow hold its ritual in hopes of bringing back
its mate? No other crow joined in its vigil. Three years later, the
solitary crow still perches but not as often.

The other pole remains empty.

#15

Once again, The Human considers the concept

Once again, The Human considers the concept of the "natural world" and keys in the words.

Google replies: "No definition found."

The Human notices that the term does not specifically mention humans. Curious to see if this is the case, The Human tries again. Ahh, this time results. *Merriam-Webster*: "all of the animals,plants, and other things existing in nature not made or caused by people." Wikipedia: "all living and non-living things occurring naturally...not artificial...all living species, climate, weather, and natural resources that affect human survival and economic activity." This suggests that humans do not view themselves as natural.("Okay" The Human thinks,) then checks the definition for natural: "existing in or caused by nature, not made or caused by man."

Not natural. Not of nature.

The Human's mind jumps to the ever-increasing popularity of alien narratives in all forms of popular entertainment and communication. In Hindi, one definition of alien is "someone who does not owe allegiance to your country."

Not part of nor bound by loyalty.

Barthes wrote, "it is language which is assertive." It is we who say and write anything to get our way; get others out of our way.

#16

When red-eared slider turtles no longer

When red-eared slider turtles no longer sun-bask—the inwardness of fall has begun. There will be no more summer-tinged days. It takes a few weeks to cease scanning for them as The Human misses the ellipsis of bodies on logs afloat their neck stretched out with abandon to receive every ray of sunlight. Lingering pleasure—publicly but unselfconsciously observed— is a rare thing. Now at the bottom of the lagoon, the turtles brumate in easeful torpor, are not fooled by massive urban artificial lighting and jam-packed schedules. Since people began "donating" their unwanted red-eared sliders, there have been efforts to capture and euthanize them. So far, they elude, persist and multiply. As do we non-indigenous peoples.

Upon moving to Vancouver, it took a few years for The Human to embrace November's copious rain and forceful, frigid winds, to be at ease with the cold-damp seeping in as soon as you step out the door. An Irish-born acquaintance shifted The Human's reaction by saying, "Ahh, but it makes everything inside so cozy." Just now The Human thinks: "A bit like the turtle's shell."

22 | The cycles of seasonal life are so evident, sometimes even shocking, around the lagoon. Increasingly, The Human longs to live like other-than-human beings.

#17

After moving into her apartment late fall,

After moving into her apartment late fall, The Human noticed a heron atop a chimney stack on a low-rise across the street. The stack had a raised grate over its opening and the heron was pressed breast down on it for days on end with no signs of nourishment. "Is it sick? Wounded? Does it need help?" None of the other low-rise stacks had herons plastered on top of stacks like this one. If it moved, it was minimally.

After many days, The Human stood at her window and called an animal rescue centre. A voicemail message outlined its service and instructed a caller to leave a detailed message. Midway through leaving a detailed message the heron suddenly rose up, flew straight toward The Human, lifting off at the last moment up over the top of her building.

Astonished, The Human interrupted herself, described what just happened with considerable embarrassment. Ended the call with, "I should have called you days ago to make it fly and avoided all this worry!"

Since then, for several blocks around, each low-rise stack has a resident heron all winter long.

#18

Second week January, The Human suddenly smiles

Second week January, The Human suddenly smiles at the sight
of the otters slipping and sliding on the frozen lagoon like five
miniature Charlie Chaplins. Then, The Human softly laughs at
the sound of "The Happy Couple" overhead. Becalmed for the
past five months, their routine duet loudly announces that mating
rituals have officially commenced in the goose world. The Human
began referring to them thus after realizing this constant honking
alarm and bickering debate was not in fact a flock of Canada
geese but the production of one vociferous goose couple. Upon
daily observation, The Human concluded that the couples'
ceaseless honking, alighting, taking flight (bickering as they
flapped), circling around and repeating it all again and again was
likely neurotic. The Human also noted the larger flock—keeping
its distance during these months—must have also reached this
conclusion.

Think of two rusty hinges or a teeter-totter much in need of oil.
Always in the lead, the female's higher-pitch honk is matched
every third beat by her pursuing male partner's hoarse replying
honk. Their ongoing squabble, their comings and goings now
a permanent counterpoint in The Human's daily soundscape.
Often, they are comic relief. Often, they remind of poignant
faithfulness. Often, they remind of insatiable human restlessness.
Longing.

And doubt.

#19
It finally happened.

It finally happened. Over the years, attempts had been made and questioned posed (to no avail); Google searches periodically done (with information out of date or too vague) but yesterday early eve, The Human (at the wheel) and friend (with map in hand) drove to the general vicinity of the Burnaby murder of crows. Drove down numerous streets to scout out the area, then parked in a relatively open area. Waited. Watched. Watched. Waited.

Quiet prevailed.

The Human had calculated how long it would take. Knowing what time the neighbourhood crows departed, the average speed of flight for crows and distance between Stanley Park and that area of Burnaby where they should be arriving soon.

A remarkable baroque sky arced overhead.

They reviewed the map: considered other location options. Remained. Waited. Watched. Occasional stragglers would pass nearby and even more occasional small groupings yet these sightings further puzzled as the crows forked: some went further south; some further north. Finally, the sound then sight of a large flock that veered off to the southwest. Into the car. Relocate. Wait. Watch. After a number of minutes, relocate a few blocks further east again.

Then it happened!

A large, noisy flock came in from the west while another surprised them by coming in from the east. Convergence!

Their destination had to be close at hand. Car. Map. Most likely spot: Forest Lawn Cemetery on a crest overlooking the city. Into the car. As they approached, crows quietly foraged on the ground.

Turning into the cemetery, hundreds and hundreds and hundreds of crows were everywhere creating a pattern of black polka dots on an uninterrupted sweep of green with embedded grave markers and well-placed trees here and there. Moving through the cemetery, hundreds were now thousands of crows resting in reverie, finding bedtime morsel snacks, basking in their collective self before the sun turned in and they moved into nearby veins of trees.

In their midst—an exquisite joy unlike anything The Human had known.

The other half of their life was no longer a _____.

#20

The Swan Lady was walking in the opposite direction

The Swan Lady was walking in the opposite direction across the street. Picture a petite, contained woman in her eighties. It had taken a year for the Swan Lady to engage in a bit of conversation. The Swan Lady was very selective about whom she would talk to yet softened when she talked with each swan. They emanated pure pleasure in her company and care.

The Human admired the Swan Lady's day-in and day-out loyalty. Regardless of the weather or her fluctuating vigour, she pulled her buggy with trays of water and grain numerous blocks.

First it was just an accepted nod or curt "Hello," then "Nice to see you," or "They are happy you've arrived." Gradually the exchange lengthened.

Today, the Swan Lady seems not herself.

Perhaps this is because the Swan Lady is not with her swans. But then, The Human recalls meeting the Swan Lady from time to time on their shopping street near by. Elegantly dressed and assured, the Swan Lady always returned The Human's greeting. Although The Human does not yet know of Thea's death, something signals The Human to not call out a "Hello!" today. Then, The Human notices the Swan Lady is gesturing urgently with one hand and addressing someone who is not there.

Lost.

The Swan Lady seems lost.

It's as if she's just awakened from a bad dream.

#21

The Swan Lady gave the swans their names.

The Swan Lady gave the swans their names. Talked quietly, lovingly to each of them. At the sight of the Swan Lady, they would glide across the lagoon to her. The operative word now has become "would."

The Human has been avoiding writing about the Lost Lagoon Mute Swans. They lived on the lagoon for many years. The operative word now: "lived"

There were two couples. Their wings were pinioned against flight and eggs addled by park staff, yet they meticulously built their platform nests amidst the bulrushes; sat and devotedly turned their eggs every spring.

This spring, one male was taken to the vet for an overnight examination, and his mate Thea was alone on the eggs.

Hunger took her briefly out on the water.

Unable to fly and with no mate to assist, she was fair game for the otters. Her feathers were strewn out on the lagoon's surface the next morning. Human lagoon regulars' distress was palpable, and the park staff relocated the other three swans to a private sanctuary "up the valley."

Weeks passed. Walking around the lagoon, The Human's brain periodically scans for where the swans are. It's automatic.

It may take a long time for the brain to accept their absence.

#22

The duel to death took place in an opening

The duel to death took place in an opening between the seven-storey high hemlocks, cedars, redwoods and maples, and the high-rises that border the park. The crows, like The Human, prefer residing in this cheek-by-jowl territory of seeming incongruity, this juxtaposition of opposite worlds where interactions are not routine and unthinking.

During the previous weeks, tension about crow hierarchy had increased. Relationships had to be sorted out before mating, nest building, fertilizations, the laying of eggs, incubation, hatching and feeding of the next generation began. Crows' behaviour was becoming the opposite of the their ease with The Human the previous fall and winter when they had become a familiar with The Human. They often flew gently down in front of The Human, turned, and with a tilt of their head queried if The Human might have a peanut for them. The flock's gathering early every evening on the high-rise across the street to fly back to their murder site in Burnaby had ceased.

In retrospect, the duel wasn't surprising: retrospect the reversal of disbelief. Crows will kill a dying crow to put it out of its misery, and will execute a disruptive crow whose behaviour puts others at risk, but the early morning uproar without diminishment for ten minutes was unsettling. Finally, The Human couldn't bear it any longer. Got up. Dressed quickly and went out to see what was happening.

Crossing the street, the wave-like intensity of their uproar was diminishing as the crows were beginning to empty out of the trees. Nevertheless, The Human entered gently. Spoke softly to them. Visually searched the ground for a black body. There was no body, no clues of what had transpired. This was odd. Just as The Human turned to leave, the sight of a perfect halo of soft breast feathers on the grass caught her eye. No other body parts: just this eerie halo. The remaining crows were still ceaselessly cawing but with less agitation and alarm.

The next day The Human returned to the kill site.

The eerie halo had been scattered by the wind.

The Human searched more carefully. Was troubled. It wouldn't have been the eagle. It wouldn't have landed. Maybe it was an owl, but it wouldn't have risked being attacked by the flock nor stayed that long. Was it a fight for dominance between two leader crows? Did the winning group take parts of the body as trophy? Or, did the crow's family take them as memorial? The Human broadened the search. Began to look further away in the taller grass.

There!

A scattering of wing feathers; a knot of intestines but nothing more.

That evening, the news detailed the renewal of chemical warfare unleashed on women and children in Syria.

By the next morning, The Human's thoughts had shifted to human warfare. It seemed far more vicious, more horrifying in its deceptiveness. The crows did not draw countless others into their fight, did not force captured children to be used as suicide bombers.

In that light—crows seemed more civilized.

#23

"When I first plied paddle across gunwale of…"

"When I first plied paddle across gunwale of a light canoe and idled on the margin, I named the sheltered little cove Lost Lagoon. This was just to please my own fancy for, as that perfect summer month drifted on, the ever restless tides left the harbor devoid of any water at my favorite canoeing hour and my pet idling place was lost…" E. Pauline Johnson

Faceted sunlight on water; words floating on the page.

Written language is a relatively new form of communication that dates back 5,000 to 6,000 years.

Lost Lagoon was known as "Ch'ekxwa'7lech, meaning "gets dry at times" (uncredited/Wikipedia); "an artificial, captive…body of water" (Stanley Park Ecological Society); "little more than a brackish tidal flat…unsightly, actually smelly" (Thetyee.ca/An Unnatural History of Stanley Park).

With the invention of written language, humans acquired the power to define and disseminate our biases, points of view, prejudices, knowledge and ignorance.

The alphabet; a set of arranged, sequential lines became the real.

Even when the humans encountered the embodied real, their written sets of lines predetermined what they saw.

#24

Recently, while teaching a group of creative writers

Recently, while teaching a group of creative writers, the
question of writer's block came up. When The Human replied:
"I don't believe there's such a thing as writer's block," they were
taken aback.

Lost Lagoon life has shed light on a related state of conscious-
ness: doubt. Recently, The Human has been considering the
difference between doubt and caution. In the class The Human
elaborated, "Writer's block is actually doubt in ourselves."

Caution is a crucial skill for wildlife survival and flourishing.
Doubt, in comparison, seems more of a human condition.

Caution, Latin. "to watch, take heed, to guard."

Doubt, Latin. "dubius, hesitating between two alternatives."

The Human continued: "If you think that your goal is to rid
yourself of doubt you will never succeed. No matter how many
books you have published, how well they have been received,
doubt will accompany your entire writing life. We never escape it.
Our confidence must be in the poem or prose narrative that has
sought us out. Chosen us to write it. Then doubt falls away."

The Human now wonders: have we lost our animal instincts for
caution—become as noosed by doubt as The Happy Couple?

#25

November comes from the word "novem"

November comes from the word "novem" (meaning nine).
It indicated the ninth month of Ancient Rome's ten-month
calendar prior to the Julian and Gregorian twelve-month calendar.
January and February did not exist for the Romans. The Human
muses: what would it be like to return to the ten-month calendar?
In an ancient brain cavern, might The Human still retain that
spring should begin two months sooner, that November taunts us
with the insistence that there's still a long haul to go before rejuve-
nation? The Human notices the shortening of the crows' workday.
During spring to early fall, they return to their Burnaby roost at
8:30 p.m. Now they head out at 3:30 p.m.

November was Blōtmōnaþ, "the month of immolation." The
month "heathens" sacrificed cattle in keeping with their "pagan"
beliefs. The Human grew up with the ritual of raking leaves and
the smell and mesmerizing sight of burning them in late fall.
Was this now-banned practice our last link to this annual time of
immolation?

#26

The Human has been reading more about crows

The Human has been reading more about crows and has deduced that it likely was owl that killed the crow last spring. The Human often feels the presence of owl. Even in the dark, senses it—spots it.

Owl accompanied Athena, virgin goddess of wisdom: saw things she couldn't see. In Roman times, an owl feather placed next to a person asleep prompted the sleeper to speak their secrets aloud. A few days ago, a dear friend of The Human died. In the night, The Human awakens as grief stealthfully takes wing at the most unexpected hours. Having just written that, The Human now pauses and reads that in some cultures, owl is the "harbinger of death." Three years ago while hiking with this friend, The Human and friend paused to chat, and The Human suddenly felt compelled to look up. Nearly five metres above them, two side-by-side great horned owls perched on a tree limb. Four sets of eyes gazed at one another for some time.

Wisdom and death.

The Human wonders if acquiring wisdom requires some kind of death—hears the great horned owl's repeated call every so often in the blanketed night.

#27

The morning they learn of their mutual friend's death

The morning they learn of their mutual friend's death,
The Human and neighbour writer friend meet for a consoling
walk. When the door of death opens, humans briefly cherish
one another more before the door closes on their loved ones'
unalterable absence. The two grieving friends walk slowly around
the lagoon. Listen, look, exchange bits of knowledge about lagoon
life. They seek out the soft pinks, yellows, and whites of fragrant
early blossoms: plum by the tennis courts; daphne by the path;
witch hazel by the bike tunnel; toothed box by the Pitch & Putt
entrance. Inhale for their friend in this here-of-no-longer-there.

Nearing the end of their walk The Human recounts the two great
horned owls story then notices three walkers stopped; looking
intently up. As they approach The Human sees it: a large eagle
nearly eight metres up on a fir limb, its immature bronze-brown
plumage startlingly radiant in the sodden-grey day.

#28

Bird life is a barometer for the lagoon

Bird life is a barometer for the lagoon. During the summer and fall-drought of 2016, all forms of wildlife suffered. Birds fell silent—flew as little as possible. Even the forest was enveloped by an eerie stillness. It was as if the very effort and moisture to produce calls or songs required too much; taxed lungs increasing effort to inhale the emaciated air too much? The air was weighty. Odourless. Humans wore masks even inside—the particles so minute even closed windows failed to protect our lungs.

The lagoon itself was steadily depleting, its water level dangerously low. With no fresh water to replenish, its colour and consistency reminded of pea soup. Its surface dull: the playful mirroring of its surrounds and sky no longer existed.

Even one of the rarely seen foot-long carp lay dead on the new shore where the water used to be. That fall and into the early spring, trees were so parched they found it hard to retain purchase in the moisture-depleted soil; they collapsed with no warning nor seeming provocation. A number of the largest ones lingered until the following summer but even then—when precipitation increased— suddenly crashed down (too depleted to recover).

The lagoon's waterfowl were also depleted. Only the Canada geese, mallards, various kinds of gulls, occasional cormorants, herons (the heronry of over 100 nests only 3 blocks away), a few wood ducks and a couple of coots mated and repopulated the lagoon. Even with the improved rainfall in 2017, the waterfowl diversity and numbers remained depleted. Widgeons, grebes, mergansers, canvasbacks, teals and scaups once again failed to arrive. Quietude also enveloped human visitors.

The dramatic changes were seldom commented on but in their restraint seemed deeply felt.

It is now February of 2018, and the usual winter ceaseless rains have returned. So, too, have the Canada geese, mallards, occasional seagulls and cormorants (taking a break from the sea), now-and-then coot and wood ducks. But a great many of the other waterfowl remain absent.

Most of the songbird varieties layer in over the weeks. Their ardent songs filling the air like musicians tuning their instruments in an inverted orchestra pit.

The Human wonders, "Are we out of the woods?" Hesitates. Feels the seductive pull of this quick-fix thinking but knows, "No, we are in the woods—more dependent than ever on one another."

#29

Morning tea in hand, gazing out the window

Morning tea in hand, gazing out the window at the large coni-
fers heralding "Stanley Park … one of the great urban parks of
the world, with 400 hectares of west coast rainforest…." After
a few minutes reverie a curious thought breaks the surface of
The Human's mind—there are two nights for every one day! One
night precedes midnight; then the remainder of that night con-
tinues until next day's dawn.

The unanticipated collapse of this false symmetry ("day and
night") stuns The Human who finds sleeptime more unpredict-
able and intensified than waking hours. Nighttime's collage of
associative memories, images, and sensations is comprised of an
entirely different logic—a logic we've little say in. The Human
then thinks of Janus, the Roman god of gates and doorways
"depicted with two faces looking in opposite directions."

The same night: p.m. looking one way; a.m. looking the other.

In the early hours of Thursday a.m. three weeks ago, a dear friend
died, the dear friend of the two owls. Each subsequent Thursday
a.m., The Human awakens for several hours. Grief enfolds. On
the third Thursday, The Human hears it.

Four hoots of a solitary great horned owl.

#30
Mid-February: two days of tender sunlight

Mid-February: two days of tender sunlight after months beneath the grey bowl of cloud and rain. The Human realizes how rare the smiles of strangers passing by or sitting on the bus have been: their smiles' sudden emergence almost blinding. A world without shadows flattens out. Now thrust into a 3-D world once again, a kind of vertigo seizes the two-legged. Upon moving to the rain-forest of the west coast, The Human struggled to adapt but has learned to relish the dampening down, the quietude of winter, the lessening of urban restlessness.

On her favourite perch at the end of the sofa by the south-facing windows, The Human circles within like a deer searching for a comforting spot to rest. The memorial for her dear friend is this week, and The Human has been asked to read an excerpt from the friend's last novel. Questions arise. Would her friend want an excerpt that represents her oeuvre? Or, would she prefer one that embodies the spirit in which she lived, or, an excerpt that gestures at her quest as a writer? It is impossible to know. So, The Human will return to a way she has learned to seek the narrative's help; she asks the book to signal her. Turn the pages without an assumption and notice when the passage leaps out; for the book knows her friend far more than she, for her friend remains held within its arms.

#31

Picture it as a slightly aberrant-shaped lima bean

Picture it as a slightly aberrant-shaped lima bean—six blocks
wide by four blocks across—with a 1.75 kilometre gravel and
earthen path hugging its shoreline, these in turn held by
conifers and deciduous trees' protective embrace. Notice its
well-camouflaged beaver lodges: one on the south end; one on
the north end. Picture its ceaseless reflective conversation with
the trees and ever-changing sky and movement of air. Keep in
mind how close it came to obliteration numerous times, the
final attempt by the Vancouver Trades and Labour Council to
get the city to drain it, fill it in and make a sports field. Whisper
a thank you to those who worked to have it officially declared as
a bird sanctuary in 1938. In the early fall notice how the Canada
geese congregate at the narrowing arm leading to the stream in
twilight. Puzzle about how strangely quiet they are, and why two
or three adults take turns paddling to where the lagoon opens,
then retreat. Paddle out. Retreat. The Human is mystified: "What
are they waiting for?" Then imagine them suddenly, soundlessly
unraveling in an unbroken line that swims as one being across the
lagoon to where they spend the night. It takes a few times before
The Human understands. The adults are waiting until the eagle
has turned in and it's safe. This choreography as eloquent as any
The Human has ever seen.

#32

Early May, The Human is on a ten-day trip

Early May, The Human is on a ten-day trip: work combined with visiting friends in Montreal and Toronto where the final winter ice and snow has melted revealing accumulated months and months of mammal and human refuse. In the monochromatic landscape, first chartreuse buds dot the bold-blue sky.

Upon returning, Vancouver's West End feels tropical by comparison.

Post mating and nestbuilding, the crows are uncharacteristically quiet; secretive. Cunning in their elaborate efforts to obscure the locations of their nests, flying one way then suddenly darting another. Around the lagoon the first goslings are ceaselessly satellited by their parents who hiss, lower their heads and swerve their necks menacingly at humans passing by while the Happy Couple's indecisive honking overhead continues.

Considering a gelato, The Human strolls into Café D'oro and sees the Swan Lady, having coffee with a friend. After chatting together for a few minutes, it occurs to The Human that the Swan Lady may possess the answer to a question about the lagoon: | 43 "Perhaps you can answer a question I've had about the lagoon: do you know how deep it is?" She immediately replies "Oh yes. It is two and a half metres deep." The Human replies. "I had guessed about that, given it was a tidal basin. I've not seen you around the lagoon for a while." The Swan Lady replies: "On no! I don't go there now—it's changed so much! There are seven otters now, and the Parks Board isn't controlling their population. They kill everything (The Human thinks of the Swan Lady's favourite

swan); that's why there are fewer and fewer ducks." She nods at
her friend: "We walk the forest trails instead and they are lovely."

Later, The Human recalls being told, by another lagoon aficio-
nado, that the Swan Lady had suffered a profound tragedy: the
deaths of two of her dearest ones early in her life. Now the lagoon
has become a place of death.

#33
Picking up the binoculars, The Human checks

Picking up the binoculars, The Human checks on the crow who
has been sitting on her eggs for the past month two stories below
The Human's apartment. The purple-plum tree, now leafed,
allows only a portal view of the nest. The mother, on occasion,
only briefly leaves the nest to stretch and groom herself on the
low-rise roof across the street. Now she perches on the rim of the
nest when The Human catches a glimpse of the yellow outline of
a wide-open beak.

A nestling has hatched!

Sheer joy currents through The Human.

Connection with the crows has become more erratic. Tenuous.
The flock no longer gathers in the early evening on the buildings
across the street to return to Burnaby. They now gather
haphazardly at First Beach and this suggests that it wasn't an owl
who killed the lead crow but rather a young rival with different
protocol.

These prospective parents below are the teenage crows that
The Human is most fond of. These are the ones whose gentle,
undulating flight approaches behind her before they land in
front, turn their heads quizzically: "Peanuts? Today?"

Another pair of the same neighbourhood flock have built their
nest in the large deodar cedar outside The Human's bedroom.
Last year, the lagoon raccoon climbed up, frightened them with
its fierceness and consumed all the eggs. This year, they built

their nest even higher. The Human mentioned the idea of putting a metal collar around the trunk of the tree (that raccoons couldn't climb) to the retired fellow next door. His response stunned The Human: "Oh no. You can't interfere with nature!"

Considering the actions of men who have profoundly interfered with nature to ever-increase their profits, his righteousness rankled.

#34

Natural light in The Human's various dwellings

Natural light in The Human's various dwellings had been sparse for many years. This deprivation was exacerbated by The Human's dislike of overhead lighting, then the replacement of incandescent light bulbs with the cold-flat light of LEDs. Eventually, The Human fled to an old low-rise with hip-to-ceiling windows. Regardless of the weather, light now infuses life and The Human is grateful daily. This morning, sipping breakfast tea, a mini-drama begins to play out in the low-rise nine metres away.

As usual, the beige-coloured venetian blinds—in the apartment nine metres across the way—are down. This morn, however, The Human sees the rarely seen oatmeal- and taupe- striped cat slip between glass and blinds, its colouration so similar to the blinds that it seems like an illusion.

Now motionless, it sits on the sill: stares up at the roof's corner.

A crow couple, having just perched about a metre above, cannot see it.

Head tilted back, cat's body is a tightly-coiled spring that trembles every few moments ever so slightly with absolute anticipation: taste of crow.

Upon landing on the roof's flashing, skillfully—like butchers sharpening knives—crows clean their beaks in their habitual sets: one side then the other; one side then the other (repeat/repeat/ repeat). Then, as they often tenderly do on this particular perch, the female pecks at a freeloader on the male's haunch but the male stiffens. Senses something is amiss? Feels danger? Ignoring his mate's gesture, he moves sideways a few inches.

Cat—transfixed—lurches slightly imagining pounce.

The female steps sideways to her mate. Leans in to groom again. He sidesteps another few inches; she immediately sidesteps toward him. This repeats seven times like a comedy routine.

Uncharacteristically, neither cat nor crows are aware of being watched.

Then suddenly, cat's head swivels toward The Human.

Immediately, it slips behind the blinds with an air of disdain.

The electricity of the mini-scene dissipates.

Crows lift off.

#35
Since moving to the foot of Barclay

Since moving to the foot of Barclay (only one low-rise building away from Lagoon Drive) The Human has been noting with increasing concern the ivy advancing up the magnificent black cottonwood on the corner of Lagoon Drive and Robson. As each year passed, The Human anticipated that whoever was responsible for, or owned that small pie-shaped property, would notice and chop the ivy down. Each year it advanced considerably higher. Now seventy-five percent up the tree, action had to be taken. In another year, possibly two, it would kill the black cottonwood. Have others noticed the ivy advancing, knew it would kill the tree, and done nothing? More and more The Human noticed this kind of inaction: shrubs and plants dying in front of people's houses and apartments but no one noticed. Or, if they did, still did nothing. Was it a case of "Oh, someone else will do it" thinking?

So, The Human took action. Began to investigate who owned the property (The city? The Parks Board? The owner of the high-rise abutting the corner?). It took a couple of weeks, but once it was determined that it was the city, the right department could be tracked down. When they cut it down, they were amazed at its size. The vine was thicker than one's arm. Gradually the vine's leaves died. The tree began to reassert its beauty again. | 49

For The Child, the cottonwood had been a rare and cherished tree her great-grandfather had planted. Four of them heralded the 259-hectare section of farmland of their extended family farms. One of the cottonwoods was at the end of The Child's family lane.

The Child loved lying beneath it, listening to the leaves sounding in the breeze. Subsequently, as an adult, one of the suttas The Human has memorized to accompany her is:

> "Cut the root of the vine that chokes the tree
> and its clinging tendrils wither away entirely.
> Sever the conventionally grasping mind
> and all bondage and desperation cease."

#36

Joy soars. Plummets.

Joy soars. Plummets.

Two days after sighting the yellow diamond-shaped open mouth of the first nestling, the crows' nest was silent. Still. No comings and goings, no glimpses of black feathers: nothing. Those months and months of mating, searching for the right nesting site, building the nest, laying the eggs, incubating them, bringing food to the female, beginning to feed the first nestling while incubating the other eggs abruptly stopped.

A raccoon or squirrel had raided the nest. Devoured its contents. The Human is dispirited yet knows how gaunt the lagoon racoons have become from nursing their young.

In the western world, the loss of a human's life typically transpires over a length of time, sometimes years. In the undomesticated animal world, it is utterly unpredictable. Seldom out of mind. Turns on a dime.

Sudden death makes death more present. Visceral. Most humans' focus is on delaying death: trying in every possible way not to die, and often denying it. (Acknowledging death is avoided like an offensive comment.) In early June, now as The Human walks around the lagoon, kill sites of plucked waterfowl feathers punctuate the shores. Fledglings are particularly vulnerable. Several days ago it was a young crow's long-shafted, short black feathers of all sizes. Two days later a female, adult mallard's plumage, yesterday an almost mature Canada goose.

Parental protection is paramount. It's evident that wood duck solo- parenting mothers are more vulnerable than the Canada geese collective daycare: on land two to three pairs guard a mixed-age flock of up to thirty-some goslings while the other parents rest and sleep. Then, when on the lagoon, Canada geese parents use a protective parenthesis: one parent in front— goslings in a line between—other parent bringing up the rear. The eagle in the towering hemlock, on the other side of the lagoon, remains on its perch at the sight of their strategy.

Here, The Human is reminded of her infant son in intensive care twenty years ago.

Birth makes death all the more real.

#37

"He's crazy as a coot!"

"He's crazy as a coot!" On the prairies, this saying always elicited a smile or chuckle. Only upon moving to the West Coast, and seeing coots for the first time decades later, did it occur to The Human most prairie humans had never seen a coot. On the lagoon, coots' takeoffs seemed cartoonish. Their extended running across the water's surface—frantic shouting—"kakakakakakakakaka-kakakakak," sounded like a mantra "will-i-make-it-?-will-i-make-it?-will-i-make-it-?" They seemed enviably unselfconscious about their anxious production. Shameless. Their small black bodies seemed like a series of commas with no period in sight.

After a couple years living by the lagoon, The Human learned that coots lack the webbed feet of other waterfowl; that explained the dramatic production of their takeoffs. On water, they pumped their heads as they swam and sounded exactly like bathtub toy ducks. On shore, they looked more like chickens strutting on oversized yellow legs and grey-green feet. Their lobed toes astonished The Human. Those toes looked reptilian, prehistoric, and spread out like the index-middle-ring finger of an open hand. More than any other bird, the coot convinced The Human of the evolution of birds from the dinosaurs some sixty-five million years ago. | 53

For the past three years The Human has noticed one coot keeps company with the mallards although so unlike mallards in build and behaviour. This coot is half their size. The Human surmised it was left behind during migration, but it has remained with the mallards throughout all the seasons for these years and appears to think itself mallard. Had it been abandoned? Orphaned?

Was it taken under wing by a mother mallard, added to her clutch?

For whatever reason, this crazy-as-a-coot emits a feeling so rarely encountered in the public world:
                    contentment.

The Beaver Lady has been mostly absent

The Beaver Lady has been mostly absent from the lagoon for the past year (due to health challenges). She has been a favourite Lost Lagoon fixture for decades. Her tightly-curled grey hair, stocky certainty, and point-and-shoot camera make her easily identifiable. Most often, she is engaged with visitors about the beavers she keeps watch over and is an opinionated source of beaver knowledge. Her devotion is inspiring. She travels by transit (a two-and-a-half hour round trip) arriving mid-afternoon and not returning to New Westminster until nightfall.

The Human isn't certain but thinks that the Beaver Lady's relationship to the lagoon beaver began at least a couple of decades ago. In conversations, The Beaver Lady has told The Human that there were a number of beavers on the lagoon years ago and that the Beaver Lady had become particularly attached to one male when he was a kit. She named him Benny. Benny would always come to her, let her stroke him and when he grew into adulthood the affection continued. Around this time, the Parks Board determined that there were too many beaver and that they were a threat to the natural lagoon habitat. They began to systematically remove them. Benny, however, eluded them. Finally, a frustrated Parks Board caretaker asked the Beaver Lady to assist. Discussion and negotiation ensued. When the caretaker agreed to relocate Benny to where they thought he would thrive, she began calling him as she always did: "Benny! Benny!" He arrived. Was immediately caged. And, turned his back on her reassurances.

Since then, the beaver population has gradually re-established itself and now there are three generations of lagoon beavers. Research about the benefits of beavers and new strategies enabling beaver and other lagoon inhabitants to easily coexist have been found. In particular, the problem of the beavers' main dam reducing the stream's fresh water flow into the lagoon has been solved. Prior, the Parks Board staff would repeatedly dismantle the dam and within hours the beavers would rebuild it. Installing a 100-millimetre pipe through the dam has enabled enough water to flow into the lagoon. And beaver are allowed to bring down small to medium-sized trees but selected mid-size to larger trees are wrapped in heavy cage wire.

At twilight, the sight of a beaver smoothly moving through the surface of the lagoon is strangely reassuring: ancient.

On the shoreline, a two-year-old beaver (accepting The Human's quiet presence) turns a tasty branch like a cob of corn. Relishing each sweet bite, its teeth make hearty, gnawing sounds. The memory of a manual typewriter—the turning of the cylindrical roller to advance the paper—and the saying, "You'll eat your words one day!" come to mind.

With beaver, each bark-word is ingested and its sculptural absence recorded on the branch.

Absence. The Human is hoping the Beaver Lady will reappear; assume her sentinel watch.

Tell her beaver stories to lagoon lovers.

#39

The fledgling crow has just begun to learn height

The fledgling crow has just begun to learn height and flight after spending its first days walking with only spurts of small flights here and there. Now it's attempting to shadow its teenage minder's lessons about higher flight. Both are standing on a favourite crow perch on the roof of the low-rise across the street. Minder lifts off and flies up a few more flights to a rectangular slab of concrete jutting out from the fashionable high-rise next door. Fledgling hesitates but emulates successfully. Lesson number one: tick!

Lesson number two. Minder lifts off again, gains altitude—banks a smooth left around the corner of the building disappearing from sight. Fledgling hesitates. Looks this way and that. Doesn't want to be left behind so lurches forward and smashes into the small window it's mistaken for sky. Falls back on the slab. Now visibly anxious about being alone on this ledge (already knowing eagle hunts here), it lurches not knowing how to read the shadow where the building juts out to accommodate a bay window. Crashes into the shadowed corner, falls backward a few feet, rights itself then dives down to solid ground again. Phew!

#40
The language of flight

The language of flight (with its unpredictable split-second changes) seems more complicated than the language of ground. All beings must learn the specific vocal and gestural language of their family over a short period of time. Survival depends on it. As does the meaning of our shared lives.

Yet ground-reading also requires an acute sensitivity: poorly-sighted raccoons stroke the ground for seeds with such sensitivity, as if they are reading braille.

We humans construct an intimate relationship via our shared language. When one of us dies, the others left behind must go through the reverse process: disassemble or set aside—one by one—all the interactive habits the relationship was comprised of, all the recalling of shared memories, telling gestures, no longer made.

#41

Upon moving here, The Human was soon mystified

Upon moving here, The Human was soon mystified by a tenderly elegant yet puzzling conifer tree on the east shore of the lagoon. Its reddish-brown, fibrous bark and needled branches signaled some type of conifer, but numerous searches through various tree books turned up a blank. Adding to the puzzlement was the curious matter of the tree dropping all its needles in the fall. Yet it didn't remotely look like a larch.

Eventually, her newly purchased *Vancouver Tree Book* solved the mystery: this tree was a dawn redwood. Yes: the needled branches looked like a redwood's but they were softer and emerged brownish-red in spring—turned green through summer months— turned reddish-brown in the fall before dropping to the ground.

Originally a conifer, the dawn redwood transformed itself into a deciduous tree in response to a radical change in sunlight patterns during the end of the Cretaceous period into the Paleocene period. Fossils told of its existence, but it was believed to have disappeared with the dinosaurs. Only in 1941 was the dawn redwood "found in a remote valley in China."

A few days ago, The Human's dear brother told her that he is dying and somehow the dawn redwood's story comforts The Human as does its gentle presence.

She goes to the dawn redwood: watches its branches float like a symphony of feathers on the breeze moving across the lagoon.

Once again, it is a time to let go. Be unmoored.

Adapt to lightness.

#42

Every so often, at this time of the year,

Every so often, at this time of the year, The Human drifts off the lagoon trail—strolls under the causeway to the Stanley Park rose garden for an opulent encounter with its sights and scents. This, too, is the season for an ever-increasing flock of tour buses full of sets of eyes that prowl the city's talking points and stare at us who populate them.

Recently, returning from the rose garden, The Human became aware of a surprising similarity.

Just as we humans construct bus, rail, car, aircraft, watercraft, office and apartment cages for ourselves, we, in turn, capture wildlife with our stares, traps, guns, cameras, poison as urbanization shrinks their habitat.

#43

Stanley Park attracts an estimated eight million people

Stanley Park attracts an estimated eight million people annually. Not infrequently, The Human is asked for directions. This summer, The Human has noticed that it is almost always the woman studying the map and asking for help while her male companion stands silently by. Just now The Human recalls how this was much the case on their family summer holidays. Her father refused to ask for directions even if it meant losing considerable chunks of time going the wrong direction. Her mother was the one who always asked for assistance. He would sit at the wheel and look straight ahead as if nothing was happening. It seemed a profound embarrassment to not know where he was; not to be efficiently in command.

Six decades later it appears little has changed—but The Human's awareness has. Now the fragility of men is so apparent to The Human. When suddenly outside their realm of knowledge, authority, they become oddly immobilized. Perhaps women are more familiar with uncertainty and having to adapt. They think nothing of asking for directions. They, in fact, become uncharacteristically forward and animated.

Just now—upon this insight—The Human notices a sorrow rising up in her chest about how little has changed.

#44

Sunlight on clear water at Julian Beach

Sun on the clear water at Julian Beach on Savary Island casts a shimmering net of light that appears to be trying to capture the receding waves. Mesmerized, The Human struggles to shift her attention to the fact that the sandy bottom is punctuated by submerged rocks studded with barnacles. Although her body immediately relaxes as she begins her swim, her mind remains vigilant. Once cut by barnacles, a swimmer doesn't ignore them. Looking down frequently, The Human notices her body relax and her eyes begin to glance down a little less frequently. Then she notices that she feels the rock before she sees it and swims easily around it effortlessly. It's as if the rock signals her before she sees it: as if its dark-cool energy can be felt. She doubts this is possible (thinks she must be imagining it) but keeps stroking without looking down to test it longer. Finds it happens again and again: each rock signals her, and she feels tender gratitude for their inexplicable kindness.

45

Often The Human has longed to enter its body

Often The Human has longed to enter its body, but swimming in the lagoon is forbidden. Its dark water inscrutable and possibly hazardous to one's health (one sign suggests). Possibly. City concerns about liability are more likely the reason. More to the point, human bathing could be harmful to lagoon aquatic life. Yet (is there always a "yet"?) there are those summer evenings when the lagoon cradles the sunset sky so eloquently that The Human aches to be held in its arms.

While The Human circumambulates the lagoon in the cooling evening, the Swainson's thrush lustily flutes up the scale to the tops of the firs.

Ecstatic: ecstatic in its entirety!

It's a wonder it doesn't fall off its perch.

#46

The tidal flat adjacent to Coal Harbour

The tidal flat adjacent to Coal Harbour (Johnson hated that name) was drained and turned into a freshwater lake by the completion of the Stanley Park Causeway in 1916. The nascent lake remained nameless until 1922 when it was officially given the name Johnson had given it: Lost Lagoon.

While musing on all this history, The Human has gradually realized that Pauline Johnson was Canada's first performance poet. Her stage performances throughout Canada, the United States and England were legendary. Her schedule fully booked for years. Johnson's Mohawk name was Tekahionwake ("double life"). Her father was a Mohawk chief; her mother English. Johnson's staged performances embodied her doubleness. Dressed in traditional, tribal wear for the first half of her show, she recited indigenous-based verse. After intermission, Johnson appeared on the stage in "fashionable English Victorian dress" and recited traditional English verse.

Her rapt audience would "weep during the recitation of one poem, and laugh during the telling of an anecdote that poked gentle fun at herself." Considering that she retired from the stage in 1909, her total theatrical transformation from one being to another must have impacted audiences as much as the special effects in Stanley Kubrick's film *2001: A Space Odyssey* wowed audiences in 1968.

By 1911, Johnson was poor; very ill. Friends rallied around her and published her stories in *Legends of Vancouver* that sold an astonishing 10,000 copies and is still considered a classic. Johnson's funeral in 1913 (a civic holiday) was at that time the largest in Vancouver history. At her request, she was buried in an unmarked grave close to Siwash Rock (Slhx̱i7lsh) in Stanley Park.

#47

Only recently did The Human find Pauline Johnson's memorial.

Only recently did The Human find Pauline Johnson's memorial.
Tucked in the shadows beneath a small recess at the junction of
Stanley Park Drive, the switchback road to Third Beach and the
parking lot for Teahouse restaurant, The Human realizes that
she has passed near it countless times but never before noticed it
despite the fact of often looking for it. Here, The Human pauses
(wishing not to offend) before acknowledging that the memorial
is strangely soulless. Reserved. So uncharacteristic of Johnson
that it mostly bewilders.

#48

Tide out, it's as if walking through an extensive library

Tide out, it's as if walking through an extensive library, the stories and natural histories of this Salish Sea coast embedded in the plethora of rocks—many configurations and composites The Human has not previously seen.

Indigenous Peoples' belief that rocks are our ancestors resonates more and more in The Human's bones.

Once again, The Human is reminded how un-storied Lost Lagoon is due to erasure and repurposing. Reminded how vulnerable a small body of water is to human whim and ignorance. Realizes how little recorded history there is; how land and water formations are disturbed beyond recognition; how little old-growth trees are left to tell the tale.

On the lagoon's north shore there is almost no visible trace of its midden. All the lagoon's saltwater life died when the causeway was sealed off from tidal life. Settler cabins were removed during causeway construction. When the lagoon was drained during the construction, the Vancouver Trades and Labour Council "adamantly opposed the idea of an artificial lake" and lobbied to have it filled in to create another sports field.

The question arises: who has the right to shape and tell the story? Destroy story?

For story decides everything else.

#49

August 5th 2018,
New York Times Magazine cover

August 5ᵗʰ 2018, *New York Times Magazine* cover: one sentence
in white font against a totally black background:

Thirty years ago, we could have saved the planet.

Early August. After just checking her phone weather app and
seeing yet another row of sun icons, The Human sighs. She has
been watching the leaves on trees and bushes curling, drying out
and dropping. Massive fires around the world are alight; some
uncontrollable.

The Human's eyes are snagged on the word "saved" on the front
page. She considers. Then recognizes how arrogant it is. How
wrong-headed; self-absorbed. And, how indifferent humans have
become to it; how that sentence should say:

Thirty years ago, we could have stopped killing the planet.

Then wonders, in the abandonment of foresight, can there be
insight? Hindsight?

A few days ago, near twilight, The Human finally caught sight
of the Beaver Lady. She was sitting on her favourite perch—a
bench—by the small pond off the north end of the lagoon where
the yearlings built a second lodge two summers ago. At first
glance, The Human did not recognize her. Her tight, white-grey

curls were straight, lifeless hair pressed to her head. Her face and body were puffy. In conversation, The Human soon learned that the Beaver Lady was seriously ill and, in addition to her symptoms, was struggling with debilitating side effects from various prescribed drugs. Her devotion to the beavers was intact; she, however, was troubled that she had had no sighting: "The mother always comes to me here but I've not seen her tonight: haven't seen the yearlings, not even the kits that are always on the lagoon by now." The Human had been puzzling about this too but persuaded herself that it was because she seldom visited the lagoon in the evening. All summer, she had only seen one beaver and almost no sight of their dining on branches and bringing down trees. As more and more weeks passed with hardly any precipitation, the water level once again shrank and shrank.

Later that evening, a Rebecca Solnit essay comes to The Human's mind. Solnit observes how the male heroic invents and monetizes digital technology (sans foresight) then, in the 11th hour when its destructiveness is no longer deniable, the male heroic invents (and monetizes) seemingly corrective technologies.

In the abandonment of foresight, can there be insight? Hindsight?

#50

It is human nature to walk in circles when

It is human nature to walk in circles when we become lost in an unfamiliar setting. And, it is common for us to be convinced we have found our way back as we near the spot where we first admitted to ourselves that we are lost. That point—where we acknowledged our lost-ness—has now become a spot of familiarity ("I remember that contorted hemlock!"). The brief comfort of this familiarity now resembles a kind of home in contrast to the utter absence of our knowing how to re-find home.

Lost Lagoon, however, wasn't lost. The lagoon was destroyed. Taken away from it centuries of Indigenous inhabitants' residence as well as those who visited and harvested its shellfish, and those who held ceremony and celebrations on its north shore. Settlers assumed that their need for easy automobile access to North and West Vancouver was an unquestionable priority.

In a recent CBC Doc 1 podcast, Rennie Smith told how her Squamish-Portuguese relatives and family had lived in a small settlement on Brockton Point from the mid-1800s to 1931. The Kanaka Ranch (a settlement of Hawaiian immigrants), the Whoi Whoi and Chaythos peoples were pushed out by the early 1920s but her relatives fought the local and federal governments who sought to remove them by proving…(they) "hadn't lived at Brockton Point long enough to have land rights…The First Nations people testified how long the community had lived there…" The courts ruled that "Indigenous people weren't reliable witnesses because they couldn't tell the time."

During Lost Lagoon's first fifty years of life, it was a playground for stock-seeded fishing, ice-skating, swimming and boating. All these were gradually discontinued due to practicality and liability as well as an increasing awareness about natural environmental protection.

As The Human writes this, she wonders—does all this loss haunt Lost Lagoon? In the past four years (based on The Human's observations) two-thirds of a wide variety of waterfowl have not returned; some of the mammals have disappeared or declined significantly in population; the main creek feeding into the lagoon has become a wetland meadow. On the other end— bulrushes, water lilies and Japanese irises have almost choked out the adjacent pond where the second beaver lodge was built three years ago. And, an increasing number of the trees hugging Lost Lagoon are noticeably stressed and dying. In nearby Beaver Lake, water lilies have almost completely blanketed the surface and reversion to wetland—which normally takes two hundred years—is transpiring in twenty.

The Swan Lady, and now the Beaver Lady (fixtures for years and years), had to abandon the lagoon. And now The Human rarely comes across the two old solitary men (one Asian, the other Slavic) who routinely scattered crumbs, seeds and kibble from old plastic shopping bags as they murmured to the ducks and geese.

So many of The Human's loved ones have died, are dying, or are seriously ill.

A poem of The Human's—published decades ago—circles like a mantra in The Human's mind:

> confronted with how lost we are narrative begins
> (our resolve) to make this place home

#51

August 2018: Once again, "Very High Health Risk" air

August 2018: Once again, "Very High Health Risk" air quality
warning for a week. Windows are closed despite the temperature;
particle masks worn inside and out (advisory warnings for people
with particular health conditions constantly repeat). Visibility
is greatly reduced. Birds seem absent, seldom seen flying; rarely
heard. People refrain from outdoor sport and as much as possible
even walking. When seen—appear to be walking in a trance.
Vancouver gains another top world city rating: the most polluted for
a week. PM 2.5 ratings are constantly checked: particulate matter
containing pollutants from almost 600 fires burning out of control
to the north and east. Particles are comprised of carbon monoxide,
nitrogen oxides, volatile compounds and trace amounts of heavy
metals, and are so infinitesimal (2.5 micrometres contrasted to a
human hair, 70 micrometres) that they penetrate even with win-
dows and doors closed.

Imagine a winter snowstorm white-out; imagine a total black-out
(the forty-eight-hour one on the Canadian northeast and U.S.
eastern seaboard in 2003—the cities completely dark—the only
movement rivers of people walking).

Now imagine this: a total grey-out for a week (sun and moon utterly
obscured).

Rachel Carson comes to mind. *Silent Spring* (published fifty-six
years ago) was dismissed, derided, and Carson was vilified by the
chemical industry and their government cronies.

While The Human has written this tale, has elation for Lost Lagoon
become elegy?

#52

The Photographer is storing equipment

The Photographer is storing equipment in her backpack as The Human approaches her on the lagoon's west path. In photography, point of view is crucial. As the Photographer nears, it strikes The Human how each of us lagoon regulars have our own version of the lagoon. Our own keyhole we see it through.

The Human has not seen the Photographer all summer. Wondered if the Photographer was okay. Considering that the Photographer was a daily regular, this absence puzzled The Human.

In the past, whenever The Human attempted brief conversation, the Photographer looked down, turned away, but today The Human is propelled to inquire: "Hello, just wondering if you've spotted any of the beaver lately?" The Photographer does not turn away. Momentarily holds The Human's gaze. "Only a couple of times; I've been coming in early morning."

This surprises The Human as lagoon beavers are twilight and nocturnal by preference, but it briefly gives The Human hope.

A month later, The Human still has not sighted a beaver. | 75

Nor seen evidence of their felling trees, nor any sight of bare branches' post-beaver bark consumption.

An image now spontaneously arises in The Human's mind: the developer bath for a photograph in the dark room. Instead of the image gradually filling in before the stopper bath, then finished in the fixer bath, the process reverses itself: the finished, sharply resolved image fades, blurs until it is gone.

#53
"The parksboard has 'trapped' the poor beavers!"

"The parksboard has 'trapped' the poor beavers!"

is scrawled in large white letters under the footbridge where their main dam had been. The operative words here: "had been."

Systematic. Late last winter, when The Human arrived one day—a caterpillar tractor had completely removed the dam.

The Human had assiduously looked for the beavers for two years; periodically inquired with other lagoon regulars but none had seen the beaver. No one except the Photographer.

In the Beaver Lady's absence, the beavers had no well-informed advocate.

Recently, The Human spotted the old patriarch by the original lodge. Other than that—there's no sign of their three-generational family.

The Human's heart sinks in her chest.

Loss seems more devastating when sensed or suspected for some time for there's the false hope that you have been wrong. Just now, looking back through this manuscript, The Human is surprised at how little the beaver are mentioned. In actuality, they were one of the mammals she most watched for; delighted in.

Shortly after, the Parks Board covered their tracks—painted over the message about the "trapped beavers" almost immediately—even though a recent 122-centimetre graffiti word (covering the other side of the bridge underpass) was left untouched.

Later, while reading *Eager: The Surprising Secret Life of Beavers and Why They Matter*, The Human is reminded that the beaver is the official emblem of Canada. In the book, The Human found out why: for 200 years, beaver were trapped for their much sought-after pelts used in European hats and outerwear. Being the major economic base for settlers, they were trapped to near extinction. Their waterways management has created most of our topsoil and their habitat provides food sources for an array of other animals.

Excellent engineers, beavers' numerous building techniques have been borrowed by humans and some of their dams have been found to be 1,000 years old.

Most wrenching is this: they are the only non-human beings to share the same defining traits we humans have: changing the natural environment to enable survival; creating a strong intergen- | 77
erational family; building permanent homes.

A couple of months later, The Human catches sight of the old patriarch: he's evaded being caught. Then a couple of more months pass with no sight of him until late fall when he has suddenly rebuilt the damn beneath the bridge where the bulldozer had removed it months ago. Its construction isn't topnotch but he's old, alone: giving it his best shot.

#54

In her ninth and final book, *Legends of Vancouver*

In her ninth and final book, *Legends of Vancouver* (1912), E. Pauline Johnson writes "These legends...were told to me personally by my honoured friend Chief Joe Capilano...and he frequently remarked that they had never been revealed to any other English-speaking person save myself."

During the course of these five years of writing *Lost Lagoon/lost in thought*, The Human has often sensed Johnson paddling soundlessly nearby yet has instinctively saved reading *Legends of Vancouver* until now.

As in many Indigenous Cultures, each of Squamish (Skwx̲wú7mesh) Chief Joe Capilano's wisdom legends sprang from a particular place such as The Two Sisters (Ch'ich'iyúy Elxwíkn - The Lions), Siwash Rock (Slhx̲i7lsh) and Cathedral Trees/Seven Sisters Trees in Stanley Park.

Johnson's faithful retelling of Chief Joe Capilano's wisdom legends is radiant.

The Human now wonders—how would we settlers, we-new-to-being-here Vancouverites, be changed if every one of us read these legends?

#55

"In the beginning was the word,

"In the beginning was the Word, and the word was with God, and the Word was God." John 1:1

In the twelfth century, the Thirteen Principles of Jewish Faith were written and the altering of 'God" to "G-d" was introduced to retain the high level of Hebrew respect yet allow the changing or erasure of the word when necessary.

O

"Around 1000 B.C., the Phoenicians and other Semites of Syria and Palestine began to use a sign in the format of a circle...they gave it the name cayin, meaning 'eye.'"

When The Human began writing *Lost Lagoon*, the vibrancy of lagoon life entranced her. Elated. The Human had no notion of how quietly-how-quickly elation could morph into elegy.

Five years ago, in #1, the question was: "The Human is at a loss for words. Considers. And, considers...is this...why The Human is a writer?"

Now the question is—can we humans meet Lost Lagoon's gaze?

LOST LAGOON

Bluestem & Bull Kelp: A Postscript

i. Tallgrass & Tall Ships

There are three things I know about my settler great grandfather.

Thing One: he immigrated to the U.S. Midwest from Norway in the mid-1800s.

Thing Two: as an old man, his hearing was so poor that my mother and her sisters would hide beneath his bed and giggle at his voluminous farts before he fell asleep.

Thing Three: as a young child I overheard my aunts recalling how in his old age, my great-grandfather's greatest pleasure was to walk down to the river two miles away and "fish with the Indians." In the early 1950s, this seemed fantastical to me as the only Indians I knew existed were in westerns on TV. In that part of the Midwest, it would be a couple of decades before the Sauk, Sioux, and Fox histories, and the devastating Black Hawk War and Treaty in 1832, resurfaced as subjects of relevance for settler scholars.

During my childhood, I also overheard a passing comment in my uncles' post-dinner conversation that the Midwest had been a sea of three-to-ten-foot-high bluestem tallgrass when great-grandpa arrived. This image provoked a strange euphoria and vertigo in me. The image of a sea of tallgrass—contrasted to the endless grid of one-mile-square sections mechanically plowed, seeded, cultivated, fertilized, sprayed with pesticides and herbicides, then harvested— was unrecognizable. When the tallgrass vanished, so did settler memory of it. In Native American memory, it remained intrinsic.

ii. Bluestem Tallgrass

Sway of the tallship my great grandfather sailed the Atlantic on. Sway of the tallgrass that he eradicated.

Found mini-essay (Roget's Thesaurus):
sway
power, 160.
influence, 178.
oscillate, 317.
be irresolute, 601.
motive, 612.
governance, 733.

Power: n. superiority, omnipotence, exertion, control.

Influence: n. upper hand, climate, knowing the right people, rule.

~~~~~~~~~tallgrass sway~~~~~~~~~

Oscillate: v. undulate, wave, swing, move to and fro.

Cross-Atlantic sailing. My great-grandfather fleeing yet another famine. Then, his journey halfway across the hundred-million-hectare swath of tallgrass swaying from Southern Manitoba to the Gulf of Mexico; from Wisconsin to Oklahoma.

Bluestem that had flourished for ten thousand years.

Be irresolute: v. be of two minds, change sides.

Did he ever have second thoughts? Waver about his actions?

Within seventy years, the bluestem was burned. Plowed under by settlers rendering Native Americans' inhabitance and wildlife homeless.

Motive: n. propaganda, pressure, hard sell, promises.

Indigenous People resisted. The Black Hawk War resulted in brutal treatment and the Black Hawk Treaty of 1832 sealed the opening of the tallgrass prairies for unlimited settlement.

70 years— 100 million hectares of tallgrass gone.

Our settler mindset: we demand ever-increasingly rapid technological change yet insist climate change will advance slowly.

iii. Bull Kelp

My love of bull kelp (and its sinuous movement) prompted me to write this essay; prompted me to find out more about the tallgrass and recognize sway in my DNA. For Salish Sea Indigenous people, like Rosemary Georgeson, kelp has remained vital.

1981. I migrated to the West Coast. Vancouver's surrounding landscape was so reminiscent of Norway's mountains, forests, islands, and sea. I began coming to Galiano; became friends with Galiano residents and authors Jane Rule and Dorothy Livesay.

It was Galiano that taught me island. Instructed me in what island is when rooted in sea. Galiano's abundant bull kelp mesmerized me with its undulating sway, its anchoring holdfast, elegant stipe, its pneumatocyst carbon-monoxide-filled bladder float sprouting many-bladed long-long arms elegant and lyrical as Matisse's naked women circle-dancing (in La Danse) And its taste? Addictive! And nutritious.

On Galiano, the thriving bull kelp forests have almost disappeared in the wake of ever-increasing tanker traffic, ferry, tourist expedition and sport-fishing powerboat traffic compounded by increased industrial waste, acidification, and the lethal effect on marine life due to ocean warming.

Governance: n. divine right, lawful authority, white supremacy, seizure of power, rule of terror.

~~~~~~~~~bull kelp sway & swirl~~~~~~~~~

Sway: v. influence, have the ear of.

In utero, hearing is our first sense to develop, and in death, our last to leave us.

Which brings me to the crucial link between us humans and the rest of the inhabitants in our natural world: our basic need for tenderness.

In the absence of an abiding tenderness, research and policy change will inevitably be inadequate, easily circumvented, and perfunctory. Prosperity will remain our rudder.

Compounding this is that within the span of just two hundred years, North Americans' place of residence has flipped from 90 percent rural to almost 90 percent urban. As a result—on a daily basis—our experience of nature is minimal and so taken-for-granted that we find ourselves saying: "It looks fine."

A couple of summers ago, during a long drought in Vancouver, plants, scrubs, trees were slowly but obviously dying. Few residents even noticed. Even fewer came to their rescue. Now, as in Cape Town—the first city of the world to be running out of water— nature reminds us we are in fact not in control.

Tender: ten-, to stretch, tendril.

As it becomes more and more apparent that old knowledges of Indigenous Peoples are invaluable, we need to give them our ear. History has proven how rapidly and radically we can change nature.

Now, we must rapidly and radically change ourselves.

Credits

"The Notebook" originally appeared in *Rocksalt: An Anthology of Contemporary BC Poetry*, edited by Mona Fertig and Harold Rhenisch, Mother Tongue Publishing Limited, Salt Spring Island, BC, 2008.

"Bluestem & Bull Kelp" originally appeared in *Rising Tides: Reflections for Climate Changing Times*, edited by Catriona Sandilands, Caitlin Press, Halfmoon Bay, 2019.